CH00656110

# DON'T BE AN IDIOT!

# Don't Be an Idiot!

Six Simple Keys to Grow Your People

Jonathan Stordy

Copyright © 2023 by Jonathan Stordy

All rights reserved. No part of this book may be reproduced or used in any manner without written permission of the copyright owner except for the use of quotations in a book review.

ISBNs:
Paperback: 978-1-80541-252-6
eBook: 978-1-80541-253-3
Hardback: 978-1-80541-254-0

For Sarah, Ciaran and Anna

# Preface

**I have enjoyed 35 years working all over the world, mainly in the drinks sector, and I believe that business can be a fantastic experience if people know how to get the best out of each other. But work can also create stress and unhappiness if the wrong management behaviours are left unchecked. I hope some of the simple keys and true stories I am going to share in this short book will help you create and find increased happiness at work more often!**

Happier people are more productive because they dedicate more *"discretionary effort"* to their company. By *"discretionary,"* I mean when the boss is not looking. These people become living ambassadors and attract people who want to work for companies with great cultures. The reverse is obviously true with unhappy people at work: more employee turnover, less effort, increased absenteeism, poorer company reputation, etc. Mckinsey published findings from a 2019 study of 1,800 large companies across 15 countries. It showed that those who invested the most in human capital by creating a challenging yet collaborative environment, as well as having a strong focus on performance, delivered the best financial results from 2010-2019. So there you have it: happier people make more money for their companies!

I am British but was born in Rome in 1962, where my parents worked for FAO from 1952 to 1980, a global United Nations organisation dedicated to tackling hunger since 1945. I have lived in Spain for the last 25 years with my family. Living in Spain was always a dream of mine, and coming here was not only a work-driven decision. I had heard my parents, John and Vicky, often tell my sister and me, *"Italy is wonderful, but wait until you get to know Spain."* They were both heavily influenced by their Spanish experiences. Vicky was born in Madrid in 1923 because her father came over from England in 1906 as Personal Secretary to Queen Victoria's granddaughter, who was to marry Spain's King Alfonso XIII. My grandfather's first day at work in Madrid was on the 31st of May 1906, when an anarchist threw a bomb from a balcony at the royal wedding cortege. The bomb got tangled up in some power lines and fell into the crowd, tragically killing 24 people. The royal couple were unscathed. What a terrifying first day at work that must have been for Albert, my grandfather, a young Englishman from Talaton in Devon.

John, my father, also fell in love with Spain in his youth. He was born in Chile in 1912 to English and Irish parents who had immigrated to Argentina and Bolivia in the early 1900s. My father survived tuberculosis in the 1930s and worked as a wartime press attaché in the British Embassy in Madrid, competing with the German embassy in the early 1940s. We wanted to keep Franco and his generals neutral, whilst the Germans wanted him to join their cause. After WWII, John returned to London to lead the BBC Radio Spanish World Service, where he met my mother, Vicky. The Spanish World Service became such an important platform for exiles of all persuasions from the Civil War to speak on air about their country. My parents never forgot their Spanish friendships. So my background is a mix of British, Irish, Italian and Spanish, which means I support England in the World Cup and Roma and Real Madrid at club level. My Spanish friends find it impossible to accept that I support multiple teams, and it exasperates them!

I started my career in the UK with Unilever in marketing in 1985. Their three-year general management graduate training programme continues to be excellent today (I think they now call it the *"Future Leaders programme"*). Detergent, food and personal care brands such as Domestos,

Magnum and Dove are sometimes not as exciting as alcoholic drinks brands, but *"fast-moving goods"* are a perfect place to learn about marketing and sales. Unilever rotate you through all departments to make you realise that what you do is only a small part of the whole operation. They also teach you in marketing that advertising agencies can only generate great ideas if your brief is crystal clear in its objectives and target market: a philosophy I have rarely encountered since.

It was at Unilever that I got a taste for international business, travelling to far-flung markets such as Jamaica, Ecuador, Egypt and the Dominican Republic to work with our local partners to launch brands. You learn a lot about local customs in developing markets, so it was a wonderful wake-up call for a 23-year-old British business graduate. For example, the Ecuadorian haircare market required tiny shampoo sachets as rural consumers could not afford a large, expensive bottle, which is unthinkable in the UK. The biggest and most enjoyable wake-up call as a smart-ass graduate was spending six months selling Flora margarine to UK supermarkets in Essex and Suffolk. I was given a really attractive brown Ford Escort. As a salesperson, and because these were the days before central order-taking, I would walk into 25 supermarket outlets a day to count the stock and place the next order on my brick-sized handheld terminal.

I learned about basic customer respect when I got kicked out of a Safeway store for not signing in properly. I had to crawl daily into the massive warehouse supermarket fridges to refund the Asda customer by counting the number of out-of-date margarine tubs. Above all, I learned how lonely the sales job can be at the coal face. Marketing sends you information about a new product launch, which is often not clear, and yet you have to generate immediate sales. I hope I remembered those lessons when I presented hundreds of times to salesforces later in my career. For me, sales remains the most undervalued profession in all board discussions I have taken part in. If the numbers come in on target, few questions are asked, but when the sales do not come in as planned, every other department has an opinion. In my view, the intellectual and emotional complexity of customer management, orchestrating promotional investments, and defending your margins and brands in the face of hostile and increasingly powerful organised customers is generally under-appreciated at board level.

I moved to work for Diageo in London in 1991, the world's leading spirits company. I have been extremely fortunate to enjoy a 30-year career in the wonderful drinks industry, based mainly in Spain but always travelling and working internationally for British, American, Russian and Spanish companies. My wife Sarah and I married in 1992 and then suddenly lost three out of four parents in quick succession, two within 24 hours of each other, for different reasons. It was one hell of a test at the start of a marriage. However, we pulled together, and our son Ciaran was born in 1994 in London – a ray of light that literally kept us going. In 1996, Sarah decided to interrupt her career as a successful barrister and leave the UK with me for the USA. I worked for two unforgettable years on Smirnoff vodka in Connecticut, where our daughter Anna, was born, our second ray of light. I liked the American business culture a lot. You can be more direct and passionate than in the UK. We needed to get away from London for a while and recover from all the loss and grief. Our two children were four and only a few months old when Diageo asked me in 1998 to move to Spain as Marketing Director, and Sarah agreed to move to Madrid from Connecticut. Thankfully, she now loves the country as much as I do.

In the 20 years between 2000 and 2020, I was firstly Commercial Director at Diageo GB (commuting Monday to Friday from Madrid), then Diageo Spain

General Manager, Beam Europe Managing Director, Russian Standard vodka International CEO and Mahou San Miguel International Managing Director. I decided to end my executive career in 2021 at 59 after five years as CEO of Grupo Agora, Spain's oldest brewery focused on Ambar beer in Zaragoza and Moritz beer in Barcelona. I am currently a non-exec board advisor helping two Spanish drinks companies, Puerto de Indias Gin and Zamora Company, working a few days a month. This decision was driven by a strong desire to have more personal freedom and family time. Sarah was extremely ill four years ago, and we came very close to losing her. She is now thankfully completely recovered, but that experience taught me that life is certainly not just about work. As time flies by, it is essential to also, at some point, wholeheartedly pursue personal and family goals.

Looking back on an international career working in such different and diverse cultures, I have realised how lucky I have been to mostly work with incredible people and be part of great teams. However, because I have worked for such a range of companies across different cultures (three multinationals and three family-owned companies), I have also occasionally witnessed some poor working environments and encountered some unpleasant and toxic people who created unhappiness for people around them. If I had stayed with only one or two companies, I don't think I could credibly conclude that the six simple keys I explain in this book can be used in any type of business. But I am convinced that, whether you are working for a large multinational or a founder-led family business, it is the behaviour of people towards each other that can generate both healthy and toxic environments. Whilst Human Resources departments, of course, play an important role in building positive cultures, growing the people around you to create high-performing teams is everyone's responsibility because people are always the key factor in business success. No amount of HR habits and procedures can be a substitute for the simple advice I want to share with you in this brief and practical book.

# KEY NO 1

## Don't be an idiot!

Everyone knows instinctively how energising and enjoyable a good working environment is and how stressful a poor one can be. So much of the difference is about managers demonstrating sheer common sense and good manners in their behaviours every day. This has nothing to do with completing annual performance assessments or sending people on development courses. It's also unrelated to having weekly or monthly one-to-one meetings and the plethora of good practices that we will touch on in this short book. If leaders in a business want to behave like jerks, toxicity spreads like wildfire. *"If they can do it, it must be okay to behave like an idiot around here."*

I love what the recently departed legendary Italian footballer Gianluca Vialli said. *"We are all responsible for our own energy."* When he died in 2022, there was an outpouring of respect for him quite apart from his footballing prowess. He was always a positive influence in the dressing room with both playing and non-playing staff. I have seen horrendous examples of bad energy and poor manners. I will, of course, never mention names in this book, but I will certainly recall stories to illustrate my points. It is so easy to create a positive environment around you every day. All you have to do is consistently do some of the following and "not be an idiot":

- Greet colleagues daily with a smile when you encounter them physically or on a call.
- Explain how a particular task you give somebody fits into the overall company goal.
- Communicate regularly how the business is doing so your people feel part of the team.
- Take time to find out something about the person that goes beyond the mere task at hand.
- Thank people for a job delivered on time or well done.
- Be genuinely empathetic when somebody suffers trauma or loss in their personal life.
- Recognise and celebrate others' achievements privately and in public.
- Have a sense of humour, whatever elevated professional position you think you are in!
- Take responsibility for your team's mistakes instead of looking for sacrificial lambs.

- Remember Plato's words, *"The measure of a person is what they do with power."*

It sounds so easy and basic, doesn't it, to follow the behavioural tips above? But common sense is actually very uncommon, and I have witnessed dreadful behaviour of the opposite kind:

- Leaders who consistently don't greet anybody but the most senior person in the room.
- One CEO would often say publicly, *"When I do something, I do it better than anyone else."*
- Another would enter a board room and ask the only female present to get them a coffee.
- Some leaders think they can interrupt others, never listen and dominate the conversation.
- Or they give feedback that totally demeans the individual, such as, *"Not good enough; do it again."*
- Others literally shout or insult when they don't get the answer they want from their team.
- Or write emails on a Friday afternoon accusing teams of *"Just not caring about my brands."*
- Poor leaders under pressure show their insecurity by looking for people to blame. They would not do that if they realised how this immediately reduces the creativity

of their organisations as people naturally become afraid of proposing new ideas.

On this last point, watch people carefully when they are under pressure and when things are not going well. Those moments are the true test of their character. Ask any professional sportsperson why they practice so hard, and they will tell you that they want to be sure their method holds up under pressure: when tension is at its highest. It's exactly the same in business. Anyone can lead when things are going well.

All the behaviours in the list above are toxic, unproductive and create anxiety in people. They usually stem from deep insecurity and selfishness. And, of course, the toxic leader loses all respect. At one of the family-owned companies I worked for, I remember a shareholder who, at board meetings, would always interrupt the presenter within the first five minutes of their presentation. As managers, we would place bets on how long he would resist before interrupting. We then ignored everything he said because he was clearly such an arrogant narcissist who adored the sound of his own voice.

So do not think that just by following HR rules and processes, you will automatically grow your people. Start every day with full awareness of the immense talent you have around you and of your personal responsibility to develop it and get the most out of it for your company. J.K. Rowling takes Plato's words on power one step further and leaves us with the following thought. *"If you want to see the true measure of a person, watch how they treat their inferiors, not their equals."* So, understand how your behaviour can release others' potential simply by being a decent human being and not *behaving like a jerk!*

# KEY NO 2

## Build muscle first

**Ninety percent of the people development courses I have attended focus too much on weaknesses, which are more politely called "development areas." I fundamentally disagree with this approach, given that this can undermine self-confidence in the individual. We are all, of course, imperfect and thankfully different from one another! Developing new capabilities in an individual is key, but never in ways that reduce their self-confidence.**

Strong leaders want their team members to be different from them. I came through marketing and sales before becoming a General Manager. Although Profit and Loss statements were always my bread and butter and contained incredible insights into brand health, I recognised that analysing balance sheets and cash-flow statements was not my natural forte. So I always hired fantastic Finance Directors I could learn from. Yet I have come across so many leaders who behave as if they are experts in absolutely everything. They are terrified of showing vulnerability and pointing to people in their team who are better than them at something. Strong leaders work hard to spot what each individual does well and try to combine different skill sets to build a fantastic team. One of the best leaders I worked for once asked each team member in a meeting to physically chart their professional and personal happiness over the past couple of years and then discuss it together. A vastly diverse set of people found themselves discussing why most of their professional and personal happiness charts went "upwards." They agreed that it was because the leader made them feel valued and let them freely express themselves, their opinions and their unique capabilities.

On the other hand, I have witnessed leaders who were insatiable in terms of their expectations of others. They were obsessive about control and never gave positive feedback that reinforced good behaviour and performance. One such family business owner was known by his people as *"The more you give him, the more you owe him."* He would constantly arrive late to meetings accompanied by his son, who was even ruder than he was. They would enter the boardroom and never greet their relatives or the executive team. They somehow believed that fear would motivate people and make people respect them. Instead, we all knew they were blocking company growth by only pursuing their own negative goals. Consequently, many talented people voted with their feet and eventually left the company. Consistently arriving late to meetings when you are the boss is a sure sign of arrogantly thinking your time is worth more than others' time.

The use of time as a symbol of power is fascinating in countries like Russia or India. I once attended a summit between two self-made, extremely talented billionaires, one from Russia and one from India. They were due to meet on the top floor of the stunning Burj Al Arab Jumeirah hotel in Dubai to discuss possible collaborations. Hilariously, both tried to impress the other by booking huge rooms on the top floor, and both arrived 45 minutes late, trying to send a power signal. Nothing came of the suggested collaboration as we never got past that initial arm-wrestle and clash of massive egos.

Imagine your favourite sportsperson or team is about to compete in the final of a major tournament. Do you think their coach will spend a lot of time reminding them of their weaknesses just before they go out and perform? Absolutely not. The majority of the messages will be about visualising success and reminding the athletes about their skills and abilities. Weaknesses would, of course, be discussed in preparation for the game, and new capability development will be worked on constantly. However, just before performing competitively, the emphasis will always be on confidence and positivity.

Possibly the best feedback I ever got from a team member was, *"You are always direct when you give me feedback about what I have to improve, but I always feel you are trying to genuinely help me and want me to succeed."* I believe that creating that *"positive feeling"* in the recipient of feedback requires true authenticity from the manager. You cannot "fake" that you genuinely care about somebody's growth. The recipient of the evaluation will sense by the look in your eyes if you are honestly trying to make them stronger and build their self-confidence.

Once you have built the individual's self-confidence by noticing and valuing their strengths, it is so much easier to work on their development areas or weaknesses. But don't just ask somebody to get better at something; show them how! Imagine a tennis coach telling a student to hit a better backhand without demonstrating how to improve their grip on the racket. Or a golfing instructor may ask you to hit the ball further without teaching you to turn your body better. Show practical examples of best practice and give people the opportunities to rehearse new behaviours. Create that positive reinforcement learning loop. Otherwise, asking to improve weaknesses is just wishful thinking, or as a Spanish friend of mine says, *"Asking turkeys to climb up trees."*

I worked for a brilliant Canadian General Manager at IDV USA prior to the IDV/UDV merger that created Diageo. He was naturally shy, but that did not stop him from giving motivating and reinforcing feedback. My team organised an annual conference and invited some stimulating speakers like the famous sports psychologist Doctor Bob Rotella, a master of positive visualisation. The event went well, and the next day we all found a sealed envelope on our desks. It was from our Canadian GM, who just wanted to say, "Well done." The same leader went on to be an extremely successful entrepreneur in retail.

The last Marketing Director I had in my team came from an advertising agency background. His biggest strengths were naturally in brand communication and innovation, but I started noticing in meetings that he possessed massive potential as a future leader. He was always a generator of constructive debate and unity in the executive team, calmly diffusing tension and helping everyone to find solutions. He also showed a natural curiosity for commercial and financial aspects. It would have been easy to pigeonhole him as a skilled brand communicator, which would have set limits on his career development. Yet, in every monthly development chat, we spoke about how he could develop his general management skills beyond marketing. For example, he could consider brands as an end-to-end business that involves manufacturing, selling and financial aspects. I also encouraged him to use his gregarious and balanced personality to learn about those aspects from his colleagues within the executive team. I am convinced he will become a great GM/CEO one day.

# KEY NO 3

## "Facta non verba."

**"Actions, not words!" As a leader, you can say all the right things publicly and complete all the standard annual performance evaluations set out by HR. Nevertheless, if your actions and behaviours do not match your words, nobody will believe you, want to follow you or be inspired by you.**

At any level of an organisation, the team leader sets the culture for their people with their actions every day. That is a serious responsibility which requires total focus. I can think of some great examples:

- Our brilliant Logistics Director at the Ambar Zaragoza brewery calmly explained to his 400 people how a cyberattack meant orders from 36,000 customers had to be processed manually as all standard order processing was compromised. People worked through nights and weekends. After eight weeks, normal order-taking through handheld terminals resumed.

- A leader who told a Regional Manager to start treating colleagues as respectfully as he treated customers, or, despite his talent and results, his future in the company would be in doubt. The manager knew that the serious warning came from a boss who believed in him and proceeded to improve his behaviour drastically.
- A CFO gathered his whole team for a virtual coffee every month to explain in detail how the business was going and take questions. This was hugely motivating, particularly for those doing crucial back-office tasks like processing orders into cash, as they can feel far removed from the front end of the business.
- A veteran Channel Director at Diageo UK was famous for hitting all his targets because he gained the trust of every key individual among his large customers, from the CEO to warehouse managers. He was also well known for how he developed several young managers within his team. The veteran was completely disinterested in company politics; all his focus was on his customers and his people.
- Another leader remained on good terms, even with people she had fired, because she explained her decisions face to face and

behaved with humanity when giving bad news.

- The global CEO of J&B Whisky made it crystal clear in the early 90s to us young Country Managers that we better demonstrate we spent 120 nights out every year in the bar trade, talking to customers and learning about the competition. He hated ivory-tower thinking, and I have never forgotten his belief in getting out to the coal face and learning from reality. This mentality took J&B to be the No. 1 Scotch in Europe before the Diageo merger and the global decision to prioritise Johnnie Walker took place.

- The owner of a famous American brewery retreated from a possible partnership because the potential investor could not tell him who would be sitting opposite his son when he died. This is such an unselfish leadership example compared to other fathers and owners I have worked with who never really pass on the baton to their children. As a result, the next generation does not develop properly as leaders and the company is held back.

- Crisis management is highly demanding and uncomfortable, but it is also a massive opportunity to grow as a leader. My biggest personal experience of leading through crisis came in my last CEO role. Six months after we almost lost my wife Sarah to a serious illness, the brewery suffered a horrendous cyberattack at the end of 2019. We did not pay the ransom, yet survived the cyberattack thanks to incredible work by our logistics and IT team. However, we were then immediately hit by the COVID crisis in March 2020, which shut down 70% of the company's 30,000 bar and restaurant customers.

- As an executive team, we held almost 100 crisis meetings during 2020. Every time, we focussed on reviewing *"employee health, company performance and future recovery."* We drastically increased simple communication across the whole company using short videos filmed on our phones and newsletters. It worked. Our owners trusted us and stayed calm during the storm as we updated them constantly. People throughout the company were absolutely amazing in their understanding and acceptance of the furlough scheme and the forced inactivity.

I can also think of some terrible examples of not *"Walking the talk."* They seem almost unbelievable, but they are all true and are excellent mistakes to learn from:

- A manager refused to attend the funeral of one of their people because *"I don't like funerals."*
- A leader denied somebody a bonus because *"They are friends with someone I don't like."*
- Another refused to pay somebody in his team a bonus *"Because that person refused to move cities when I asked them to do so two years ago."*
- A French CEO went to the funeral of an employee's son years ago in Madrid and then said in a meeting, *"Why do Spaniards cry so much at funerals?"* Zero cultural empathy!
- An owner kept the whole team waiting nine months to receive their annual bonuses.
- An owner would keep people waiting weeks for holiday approval and would ignore emails and phone messages for weeks.
- A CEO complained to me that one of my Commercial Directors *"Dresses too well."* (Yes, I promise!)
- A Regional President arrived so hungover at a team meeting in Paris that he could not speak.
- Another leader asked his sales team to get his son on the guest list for a top nightclub.
- A CEO totally ignored a competitive threat by frequently saying publicly, *"They are simply lying about their results and copying us."* And

the competitor kept on stealing market-share every year.

And yet none of these leaders thought these behaviours were remotely demotivating or negative for their teams. Some treat power as a licence to do whatever they like, particularly if the company culture allows them to do so and there are no negative consequences for toxic actions.

# KEY NO 4

## Set goals and get out of the way

**People grow fast when given clear responsibility and resources and when they know exactly when and for whom they have to deliver. As the great Quentin Tarantino said about what it takes to be a great film director, "*It is your job to have a vision and then to hire talented individuals who understand your vision. You don't have to know about engineering, lighting, costume design, etc. That is not your job! Hire great people and let them express your vision with their skills.*"**

Soon after I started my second role as a General Manager, our Marketing Director gave me some great feedback. "*Jonathan, I know you were once the Marketing Director, but that was yesterday. Let me do my job; wait for the results you have asked me to deliver and stop micro-managing me.*" At first, I was surprised and, quite honestly, I felt a little put out! But it was exactly what I needed, and I went back to waiting for our monthly catch-ups, giving her the space she deserved. Sure enough, she and her brand team launched one of the most successful gin innovations in Spain, Larios 12.

Of course, it can feel scary to set somebody's objectives, stand back until the next meeting and wait to be pleasantly surprised. However, many burned-out and exhausted leaders suffer from the *"control freak disease."* Instead of doing their own strategic roles, they feel more involved by checking up on their team's work in an obsessive way.

One of the best bosses I had really made me raise my game when he first listened to me complaining about how we were struggling to deliver a crucial Smirnoff advertising campaign in the mid-90s. He stood up, started to walk out of the office and left me with the following words, *"Who is the Marketing Manager?"* It made me realise I was in charge and simply had to deliver for him!

Another time I felt totally energised and inspired by a leader was when I had just finished my training period as a Management trainee back in the day at Unilever. My boss called me in to say, *"Enough of the training, Stordy. Pack your bags and fly next week to Cyprus to lead a Brand launch with your production colleague."* I felt 10 feet tall and ready to give everything I had to represent my company in Cyprus because he was so clearly handing responsibility to me. That leader went on to create and run one of the most successful strategic marketing agencies in UK history.

One of the best examples I can remember of a leader standing back in support of their team occurred when we fell out commercially in the UK with Tesco. It was whilst I was leading the European division of Beam, an American spirits company that had recently bought household Brands like Teachers whisky, Larios Gin in Spain, Harvey's Bristol Cream and Laphroaig whisky from Allied Domecq. At the time, Tesco was responsible for 30% of all spirits sales in the UK supermarket trade. They wrote to our UK Managing Director to tell us what our new selling prices to them had to be the following year, knowing perfectly well a customer cannot legally unilaterally demand a reduction in buying price!

We decided to stand our ground, refused to buckle and told our head office in Chicago that Tesco would surely throw out all our brands for at least the next six months. The International CEO stood back brilliantly and supported us 100%. The customer saw us all completely aligned, and so we were back in with Tesco on our terms within three months. Looking back, I wish I had written to the UK Office of Fair Trading with that Tesco letter. They got found out a few years later, in 2017, for booking supplier discounts in their profit numbers before they were actually agreed. Three senior Tesco executives stood trial for overstating profits, citing an internal culture of "*fear and tension*" that had pressurised them to "*pull forward*" income. This was clear evidence that culture affects business results.

# KEY NO 5

## Measure results and behaviours

**Standing back and managing your people by objectives does not mean relinquishing responsibility for them! Monthly reviews of results and behaviours are incredibly important to reinforce success or get back on track. Behaviours are extremely difficult to change, so tough decisions about staff must be taken and never avoided.**

Possibly the best example I have seen of relentless and passionate coaching is a Spanish retail director in one of my teams. He regularly travels the length and breadth of the country to sit down face-to-face monthly with each of his key people. He delivered a complete transformation of our performance because every individual delivered radical improvements in pricing and innovation. Yet, in my experience, only 50% of leaders sit down with their people once a month to review performance, give feedback and invite it. This means that many staff members have absolutely no idea of what their boss thinks of them, and annual evaluations can be a total surprise.

One of my funniest but also ridiculous feedback experiences was in a multinational company when my boss literally left a post-it note on my desk with one sentence written on it. When I asked my manager to clarify, he said, *"Oh, yes, a colleague of mine mentioned the feedback to me, so I thought I would just pass it on."* The feedback was that *"Jonathan must not physically pat fellow managers on the back. It's acceptable in Spain but not in the USA."*

I am aware that in business, most of us are trained at some point in managing people, setting objectives, and giving and receiving feedback. But as I talk to friends and family in other industries (banking, legal and entertainment industries), I often learn that there is absolutely no management culture and no training whatsoever in terms of developing people. No wonder we hear of an abundance of *"burn-out"* and stress in those environments! I have, for example, lost count of presentations from bankers when the senior people stroll into the meeting room, say a few words and then point to a huge book that they place in the middle of the table. Every time I see the "book," I think of the poor analyst who has been up all night preparing the info very few people read and isn't even invited to the meeting to see the reaction to their work. It is a staggeringly archaic model that nobody in investment banking seems to challenge. On the other hand, surprisingly, I hear about a significant emphasis on interpersonal skill development in some of the giant tech companies. In one of those tech giants, employees get automatically-generated opportunities every month to give feedback to their managers when they open their laptops. Plus, an individual cannot get promoted unless they can demonstrate many examples of cross-functional collaboration outside of their area. Great practices!

Getting your team member to prepare the brief agenda and follow up with concise minutes of the monthly "catch-up" is a really healthy discipline. You have to be relentless in reviewing performance and giving feedback on "observed" behaviour. Giving feedback based on "*I hear from others that you failed to help that project team the other day*" must not be allowed. You have to witness a behaviour yourself if you want to earn the right to comment on it. Third-party feedback can be twisted for a host of reasons and, therefore, can be unfair.

Professional discussions about a particular business opportunity are generally straightforward as they involve mainly exchanges of opinions based on facts and experience. Imagine, for example, you are reviewing a recent acquisition, a relatively new brand launch or a set of financial results. The metrics help to generate a logical exchange. Things become a lot tougher when we enter a discussion about behaviours.

For example, I once had a talented Commercial Director working in my team who I promoted. He consistently displayed an excellent focus on performance but struggled to work collaboratively. His development area was learning from his peers and celebrating the successes of his own people. In many of our monthly reviews, we would discuss this tendency, and he would promise to learn the lessons. He is still young, and I really hope he develops well in these areas. Otherwise, he will find it challenging to realise his tremendous leadership potential.

Another HR Director in one of my teams was smart and capable in all the technical aspects of his profession. This included setting up development programmes, helping to generate and review company values with culture surveys and managing the "darker side" of HR, such as organising payroll and supervising dismissals. But he struggled to exemplify company values in terms of, for example, avoiding snap judgments of people based on only cursory interactions. Time and time again, we would talk about this, and like the Commercial Director mentioned above, he would vow to change but repeatedly failed to do so. As he rightly said himself, *"People have to change their core beliefs to change their behaviours,"* and he simply has not been able to do that yet.

When I look back at my executive career, there were times when I took the hard decision to remove an individual from one of my teams after failing to address a development or performance issue on several occasions. It is never pleasant, but it absolutely can be done fairly and correctly. On most occasions, that person goes on to be more successful and happier in another environment. However, at other times, I think I gave some people too many opportunities and was too generous with them, which did not set the right example for others. Getting this balance right is probably one of the toughest jobs for a leader!

# KEY NO 6

## Your only lasting legacy will be the people you grow

When you reach the end of your executive career, you look back and realise that most of what you remember and genuinely value is all about the people you have worked with. The great brands I have worked on will always have a special place in my heart, and drinking them every now and then is a real treat. Yet we are merely temporary custodians of their fabulous history, as they will last far longer than any of us. Whereas remembering people you have worked with and hopefully helped to grow gives you the biggest permanent smile. Like me, you will also be grateful to the many great leaders who gave you opportunities and shared their experiences with you.

Try this yourself now at whatever stage you are at in your career. Do you remember the set of financial results from ten or even five years ago? Or do you instantly smile (or grimace!) when you think back to a particular colleague or a leadership situation involving people several years ago?

I am certain that there were many times I did not live up to all six keys I have set out in this short book! But overall, I am proud of at least consistently trying to do so and of the people I have had the good fortune to learn from and influence along the way.

In summary, this short book is about using real stories from my experience to demonstrate that taking responsibility for growing your people is a crucial factor in business success. It is not a "soft" issue that can be outsourced to the HR department or forgotten about when short-term business pressures appear. Success in this area is hard-wired to short and long-term business growth. The most significant part of people management is common sense. Hiding behind compliance with standard HR practices can never replace your own daily positive behaviours. But if you care passionately about your people and their professional and personal growth, you will have the maximum positive impact on your business as a leader. That will also be the most valuable legacy you will leave behind for others and for yourself at the end of your executive career.

Stay close to leaders who manifest the positive behaviours I have described, as you will be happier and you will develop better and faster. Fortunately, inspirational leaders who genuinely care about growing their people outnumber the corporate politicians who exist in the real world and step on others to get what they want. The respected British ex-politician David Miliband points out that in global politics, *"We live in an age of impunity,"* so we should not be at all surprised that impunity can, at times, reach the workplace. I am afraid that corporate politicians do thrive, particularly in company cultures which allow the pursuit of power to become an abuse of power. When you encounter these people, stand up to them assertively. It might be a good idea just to hand them a copy of this book and ask them to read and discuss their thoughts! In pushing back against a bully, I love the model I once heard from a Spanish occupational psychologist who came to the brewery and said, *"Be neither aggressive nor passive, be assertive."*

I hope leaders and managers in all kinds of companies and at all stages of their careers use this book as a practical aid for growing their people, and it helps them to be happier and more productive!

Finally, a massive thanks to the dozens of leaders who have given me opportunities and patient coaching along the way. I hope I have passed on just a small part of everything you taught me.

Printed in Great Britain
by Amazon

41651833R00027